This book is dedicated to Dr Cherry Collier. I would have never written it, if you didn't get me to realize my potential as an author! Thanks for seeing the best in me and beyond.

- Shanti "Shoestring" Das

Thuy-An,

So great seeing you in NY at the WEEN awards!

Continued blessings,

Shanti

"SHANTI AND I SPENT EXTRAORDINARY YEARS AT LAFACE RECORDS DEVELOPING THE CAREERS OF TONI BRAXTON, TLC, OUTKAST, PINK, AND USHER TO NAME A FEW. IT WAS AN INCREDIBLY IMPORTANT TIME, NOT JUST FOR US BUT ALSO FOR THE TEMPLATE THAT LAFACE ESTABLISHED FOR THE ENTIRE MUSIC INDUSTRY. SHANTI HAS GONE ON TO CARVE OUT A CRUCIAL ROLE FOR HERSELF IN THE ENTERTAINMENT INDUSTRY. SHE IS AN ORIGINATOR, AND I AM THANKFUL THAT SHE HAS DOCUMENTED HER AMAZING HISTORY FOR ALL TO LEARN FROM."

## - ANTONIO 'L.A.' REID

"SHANTI DAS IS A LEGENDARY FIGURE IN THE RECORDING INDUSTRY. HER VISION AND COURAGE HAVE CONTRIBUTED GREATLY TO THE QUALITY OF MUSIC IN OUR TIME. DON'T MISS HER POWERFUL BOOK ON HER LIFE AND WORK!"

## - DR. CORNEL WEST, PRINCETON UNIVERSITY

"I BELIEVE THIS MIGHT BE THE ONLY LITERATURE OF ITS KIND THAT DELVES INTO THE TRUE LEVEL OF COMMITMENT THAT'S REQUIRED TO MAKE IT IN THE ENTERTAINMENT BUSINESS. I LOVE SHANTI'S HONESTY AND CANDOR IN ALLOWING READERS TO SEE THE UPS AND DOWNS THAT MAY OCCUR WHEN AIMING FOR YOUR DREAM, YET IF ONE STAYS FOCUSED, THEY CAN SOAR."

## - MC LYTE

"SHANTI HAS BEEN PIVOTAL IN THE EXPOSURE AND GROWTH OF OUTKAST SINCE DAY ONE. WHEN SNIPPET CASSETTES AND RECORD STORES WERE STILL AROUND, SHE WAS RIGHT THERE TELLING WHOEVER SHE COULD TELL ABOUT THE MUSIC. IN THE OFFICE AND IN THE FIELD, SHE HAS ALWAYS BEEN ABOUT THE WORK. I CAN'T BEGIN TO IMAGINE WHAT IT MUST BE LIKE TO BE A WOMAN IN THIS BUSINESS, BUT I DO KNOW SHE HANDLES IT WELL."

## - ANDRE 3000 (OUTKAST)

"SHANTI DAS' INSIGHT IS NOT SOME SCATHING TELL-ALL, IT'S ACTUALLY AN INFORMATIVE MANUAL ON HOW TO COME UP IN AN INDUSTRY THAT HAS PROVEN TO BE SHADY!"

## - Q-TIP

# CHAPTER EIGHTEEN
## "ON TO THE NEXT ONE"
### (Always Have a PLAN B!)

ay-Z and Swizz Beats delivered a banger with "On to the Nex One!" Swizzy said, "I got a million ways to get it, choose one –eh pring it back, now double your money and make it stack!" And Jay said, "I don't get dropped, I drop the label!"

Well, ladies, you can't branch out on your own and drop your situation unless you have a plan B! In the age of e-mail, texts, fb and tweets, it's easier than ever to multi-task and have side-hustles. Now don't get me wrong, you don't want to be a "jack of all trades and a master of none." It's important to be passionate about one thing when you first get in the game and to perfect your craft. But after you've been in for a while and experienced success in your position, it's okay to diversify.

You don't want to have your back against the wall if you ever get laid off or fired. Another one of my colleagues, Eric Nicks, had a great saying that is fitting for this chapter: "Don't get caught without a chair when the music stops!"

One of my first real side-hustles came about when I co-founded R&B Live New York. We had a great run in the N-Y-C for more than a year and a half. So much so, that other major markets followed sui and tried to emulate what we had built. We had incredible acts on stage such as Fantasia, Akon, Neyo, and many more. That showcase reconnected me with every major label head/rep, video channel exec

artist, and then some. It created new value for my brand and brought in some extra income that I could double and stack.

That extra cushion really helped. I knew I didn't want to live in New York much longer, and I wanted to be closer to my family in Atlanta. My mom was ill, and I'd been going through a few health issues. So, I stepped out, took that leap of **faith** and quit my EVP job at Motown in  November 2009. I was "on to the next one," as the saying goes. It was a scary decision to have to make. But, thankfully, I maintained great relationships, had a few side-hustles going, and figured out a way to make it work for me.

People thought I was crazy for walking away from a top spot and a Big Boy Benz Coup salary. Now, I know my equity in BRAND SHANTI DAS, and I'm gonna make it do what it do!  I am back in "hustle mode" like 1991! I am writing several books, doing marketing and entertainment consulting (www.PressReset.me), pitching a sizzle reel for a new TV show, managing the "ATL Live on the Park" music showcase, mentoring young girls for Susan Taylor's National CARES organization, engaging in more charity work for various organizations and also running my very own foundation "May We Rest In Peace," a Non-profit that raises money to help bury loved ones whose families can't afford the funeral costs. We have laid to rest 30 people in Detroit so far, and will be expanding to other cities in the near future. The difference is—I am now thinking as an entrepreneur and philanthropist.

**GOD IS GOOD ALL THE TIME, AND ALL THE TIME GOD IS GOOD! I AM FINALLY GETTIN' MY SUZANNE DE PASSE ON, AND I AM WELCOMING ALL THERE IS TO COME!**

Don't be afraid to press YOUR reset button! In the words of Russell Simmons, "thank you" (for reading), "good night and God bless!"

- Shanti "Shoestring" Das

To my Lord and Savior - thank you for walking beside me every step of the way. I am nothing without you.

Thank you to ALL the WOMEN that have inspired me directly & indirectly. I SALUTE U!

- "Mama" Gloria Das – Thank U for birthing me, loving me and instilling core values in me. I thank GOD for allowing you to still be here with us after our recent scare. I LOVE YOU!
- Lillian "Mu" Lawson – Thank U grandma for teaching me the ropes when I was younger. Love and Miss you much! (R.I.P.)
- Anjali "Maria" Arnold – Thank U for being my big sister, role model, inspiration, financial advisor, emotional counselor, spiritual advisor, career coach, but most of all, my BEST FRIEND! I LOVE YOU! You are ONE of a kind! I would not be where I am without U!
- Sandra Lipscomb – Thank U for always being there to support me through the good and bad times. I can always count on you to listen but to give me honest and constructive advice. I love you!
- Rhonda Wade – Thank U for the support when I was growing up and encouraging me to spread my wings and fly!
- Vivian Crawford – Thank U for the love & advice over the years!
- Geri Das – Thank U for the love and good times! You are a great sister-in-law!
- To my nieces Ashtah, Chloe and Anjali – I LOVE U guys as if you were my own and I will ALWAYS be here for you! Continue to make me a proud Aunt!
- To Lillie Bell, Lurlene, Myra, Michelle, Sharon & Alexis – I am happy to be a part of the family. Thank U for supporting me since I was 6!
- To Nise & Janet – Thank U for being special "big" sisters in my life
- Dr. Cherry Collier – Aside from being a BFF, Thank U for making me remove my blindfold, so that I could see my future and write this book!! Love ya!
- Cherry Collier-Jackson – Thanks for being like a mom to me for the

• Mona & Tisha – Thank U for opening your home to me almost 20 years ago and making me a part of the fam!

• Dr. Shirley Kilgore and the late Shirley Cathcart – Thank U for being the best teachers and role models a girl could ask for!

• Bette Hisiger – Thank U for being an amazing friend to me in New York! I will always be here for you!

• Shout out to my cousins: Donna Ann Wilson Bennett, Leila Reed, Sharon Cusmano, Robin Wilson, Tennielle Benjamin Bailey, Yolanda Stephens, Barbara & Rachel. Thanks for the love!

• April Nichols - Thank U for helping me pull the book together! You are so creative Abril!!

• To my BFFs, LOVE you ALL: April, Quibulah, Cherry C, Shante, Jackie, Sharliss, Eva, Leshonda, Minka, Shelley, Nikki, Tionne, Kim, Mo, Leslie, Chiquita, Marci, Kibibi, Tatia and Phyliss (R.I.P.). I appreciate all of the support that you guys have given me all of my life!!

• Jayne, Sophia, Dawn, Lisa, Chandra, Dr Traci, Mari Jo, and Deb – Sista Friends!

Professional Inspirations:

• Dee Dee Murray - Thank U for holding that spot for me at Capitol Records even though I thought I was going to intern at the Arsenio Hall show; glad my mom didn't let me go to Cali that summer! Love u!

• Martha Thomas-Frye – Thank U for keeping it real with me and teaching me early on the ins and outs of the business! Love U!

• Tina Mauldin – Thank U for lookin' out in the late 80s and all of the 90s as I was trying to get in the game.

• Lisa Cambridge-Mitchell and Davett Singletary – Thank U both for supporting me at LaFace and encouraging me to move to marketing!

• Sheri Riley – Thank U for the many years of pushing me to embrace the brand Shanti Das!!!

• Sylvia Rhone – Thank U for blessing me with my EVP stripes and for supporting me at Universal Motown! But most of all, thank U for understanding my need to transition home. It was a very difficult decision and your support helped tremendously!

- Susan Taylor – I am so grateful to have met you this past year! You have inspired me, and so many women across all walks of life! Thank U for encouraging me during my transition home and thanks for the advice about my writing career!
- Oprah Winfrey – Although we have never met, Thank U being a shining example of excellence for women all over the world!
- Gail King – Thank U for the encouraging words you gave me about writing!
- Suzanne DePasse – Thank U for being a great role model. I have admired your career in entertainment since I was a little girl! Let's do that panel at Syracuse!!!
- Nancy Cantor – Thank U for being an amazing role model and taking Syracuse University to new heights!
- Joanne May – Thank U for advising me while at SU!
- Angela Robinson - Thank U for paving the way for women at SU to excel in the Newhouse School! Much love to u!
- Samantha Marshall - Thank U for seeing my vision as an author/literary partner. Next up Press Reset!! Love ya!
- 135th Street Agency - Thank you ladies for all that you do!!
- Wendy Eley – Looking forward to our new TV ventures!
- Lisa M. Borders, Ladi Drew, Liz Flowers and Lynn-Anne Huck – So excited to work with this dynamic team of women!
- Melantha, Chelsea P and Chelsea, Shonda Mc, Aviva and Kyoko – Thanks for assisting me through the years at the various labels. U guys rock!!

Thank you to ALL the MEN that have inspired me directly & indirectly. I SALUTE U!

- Ash Tosh Das – My biggest regret is that we never got to meet! R.I.P. Daddy, I Love U!
- Shoky Das – Thank U for being the best big brother in the world! Thanks for helping mom when we needed extra cash while I was in college and for teaching me to respect myself and to demand that respect! I am always here for U and love you!!!! My sports connect for life!

• To my uncles J.P., Louis, John – you were like fathers to me and I COULD NOT have made it to where I am without you. Thanks for taking me to school, fishing, ball games, out to eat, talking mom into letting me go to SU, the financial support and most of all the LOVE. I miss you all so much! R.I.P. guys!

• Uncle Walter – Miss u much! R.I.P.

• To my nephews Kyle, Chase & Asante – I love you all as if you were my own and I am always here for you! Keep making me a proud Aunt!

• Bobby Arnold, my brother-in-law, but really you are my other brother!! Thank U for all of the professional advice and sports memories over the years! You always give honest & helpful information. Love ya!!

• To Charles L, Chuck, Jamaal, Ronald, Travis B, Mike B, Kenny, Kevin, Billy & Cousin Donald (R.I.P.) – luv u guys!

• Coach Mac and Coach Otis – Thank you both for allowing me to be a football/basketball trainer in high school and learn the disciplines of hard work and determination from the team!

• To my closest male friends thanks for always holding me down: Jarrell (R.I.P.), Daryl, Stacy, Roderick, Charles, Chris (Stay Up!), Bernard, E Nicks, Craig, Sincere, Chico, Alex S, Chad E, Skeeter, Zane, Derek, B Hill, Greg W, Sean N, Marlon A, Stephen A, DL, Vinnie Pop, Arp & Rod


Professional Inspirations:

• Ray Boyd – Thank U introducing me to Dee Dee/Keith and teaching me the radio game.

• Keith Frye – Thank U for believing in me at Capitol and for getting me that interview at LaFace! I hope I made u proud Pappa Smooth!!

• Wayne K Brown – Thank U for the scholarships at Syracuse!

• Robert Hill, Larry Martin and Dr Smith – Thank U for being role models and for believing in me at Syracuse!

• Antonio "LA Reid – Thank U for giving me my first full time job in the game! You were a great role model and always taught me to strive to be the absolute best!! LaFace was an amazing company and the memories there will never be forgotten!

• Greg Street – Thank U for always supporting Shoestring and my projects.

• Sincere Thompson – Thank U for inspiring me back in the day! I appreciate you introducing me to all of the NY DJs and helping me get into the mixshow game!

• Donnie Ienner – Thank U for believing in me at Columbia/Sony. You are a great leader. And thanks for allowing me to work with PRINCE!

• Kevin Liles – Thank U for always taking my calls, being a mentor and for helping me to realize the need to keep my brand hot!

• Professor Rezak – Thank U for allowing me to mentor your students in the Bandier program at SU! Much love to you and Linda!

• James Andrews - Thank U for assisting with my web development for PressReset.me!

• Devyne Stephens – Thank U for giving PressReset.me a shot. Looking forward to The Future!

• Charles Suitt - Thank U for believing in me as an author!

• DL Warfield - Thanks for designing an amazing book and cover! I really appreciate all that you do!

Marlon Nichols - DNP Productions! Glad to be your business partner, let's get it Zane!!

• And to Prince, New Edition and Michael Jackson – Thank U for the incredible music you contributed to the world during my childhood years! I owe my love of urban and pop music to U!

*And lastly, thank you to everyone who endorsed this book:*
Dr. Cornel West, Antonio "LA" Reid, Diddy, MC Lyte,
Steve Rifkind, Sylvia Rhone, Q-Tip, Erykah Badu , Kevin Liles,
and Andre 3000!

Book Design, Cover & Back Photo by
DL Warfield   www.dlwarfield.com

The Fam: Lurlene Arnold (cousin), Gloria Das (Mom), Shanti, Maria Arnold (sister), Geri Das (sister-in-law)), Bobby Arnold (brother-in-law), Shoky Das (brother) and Kyle Arnold (nephew)

My nieces/nephews/cousin: The JOY of my life!! – Ashtah, Briana, Asante, Anjali, Kyle, Chase & Chloe

Shanti in Dallas at the NBA Cares All-Star Day of Service

Ryan Glover, Lisa M. Borders, Devyne Stephens, Mayor Kasim Reed, Shanti and Karyn Greer at the Happy Hour

"I'VE KNOWN SHANTI SINCE WAY BACK IN THE DAY, AND SHE'S ALWAYS HELD MY UT-MOST RESPECT. THAT'S BECAUSE SHE'S ALL ABOUT HARD WORK AND INTEGRITY. SHE BUILT UP HER OWN PERSONAL BRAND BY GETTING HER GRIND ON AND DOIN' WHAT SHE SAYS SHE'S GONNA DO, NO EXCUSES. SHE'S A RARE BREED -- NOT JUST IN THIS BUSI-NESS, BUT IN ANY OTHER INDUSTRY. KIDS TODAY ALWAYS WANT TO FIND SHORTCUTS TO THE TOP, BUT SHANTI'S A PROPONENT OF PLAYING YOUR POSITION AND GETTING IT DONE RIGHT, NO MATTER WHAT IT TAKES. WE NEED MORE VOICES LIKE HERS TO GET THAT MESSAGE ACROSS TO OUR YOUNG WOMEN AND MEN. SO TELL IT, SHANTI!"

## - DIDDY

"ALWAYS CREATIVE IN HER APPROACH WITH ONE EAR TO THE GROUND AND THE OTHER ON THE KICK AND SNARE , THIS BGIRL (SHANTI) GONE PUT SOMETHIN' WITH SOME-THIN' AND MAKE IT HAPPEN!"

## - ERYKAH BADU

"SHANTI DAS IS A DYNAMIC WOMAN AND MUSIC EXECUTIVE. HER TENURE IN THE MUSIC INDUSTRY IS THE RESULT OF PASSION, KNOWLEDGE, AND PERFECTION OF HER CRAFT."

## - SYLVIA RHONE

"SHANTI IS THE EPITOME OF DREAMING BIG & WORKING HARD . SHE IS NOT JUST A GREAT FEMALE EXECUTIVE BUT A GREAT EXECUTIVE, WHO HAS MADE MAJOR CONTRI-BUTIONS TO THE INDUSTRY. HER STORY SHOULD LAY AS AN EXAMPLE FOR YOUNGER GENERATIONS & HER SUCCESS SHOULD BE CELEBRATED!"

## - KEVIN LILES

"THE GREAT THING ABOUT SHANTI IS SHE UNDERSTANDS THE ART OF HIP HOP AND UN-DERSTANDS THE BUSINESS OF THE MUSIC BUSINESS.  SHE KNOWS HOW TO WALK THAT FINE LINE VERY WELL... NOBODY IS BETTER!"

## - STEVE RIFKIND

# INTRODUCTION:

Over the years, I have worked with artists who represent multiple genres: urban pop, hip-hop — you name it. Just about everything I have done in music has involved some kind of crossover in styles. So you might ask, "Why call yourself The Hip-Hop Professional?'"

Because it was my destiny. I was born in 1971 and grew up in Southwest Atlanta (S.W.A.T.S.) · yes an APS (Atlanta Public Schools) baby. For that very reason, I could not help but listen to hip-hop. In the movie *Brown Sugar*, Sanaa Lathan asked Taye Diggs when did he first fall in love with hip-hop? I would have to say I first fell in love with hip-hop when Grandmaster Flash & the Furious Five and the Sugarhill Gang came out. My favorite songs were "Rapper's Delight" and "Scorpio." Those two groups were F-R-E-S-H! In the 80's, I went on to discover Run DMC, LL Cool J, Whodini, and many more. One of my very first concerts was the Fresh Fest and Jam-A-Tron at the Omni in ATL. I loved the beats and melodies in the music. The South was also big on "booty shake" music, so I always had an Edward J mixtape in the cassette deck (yes, I come from an era before CDs). I really loved to dance when I was young, too. My homegirls and I formed a dance group called "Lady Silk." We actually placed in several talent shows in high school (YEEK!).

This was already embedded in my DNA. Hip-hop was me. I grew up in the culture. It was a part of my environment and it wasn't something I had to learn because I lived it every day! As hip-hop evolved, so did I. I became more focused on winning and achieving my goals. In the 90's, hip-hop started to experience commercial success like never before, and big corporations set in to capitalize on the genre. By then I was in college, and I knew I had to have a piece of the dream. I got my big break in '93 and I never looked back!

So having worked in other genres, why focus on hip-hop as an area of expertise? Well, the one thing you can say about hip-hop is that most of the lyrics come from

the heart. Rappers rap about the environments they are from and there are valuable life lessons in this music. We just have to know how to decipher the negativity from the positivity. Early on, hip-hop taught me about the struggle and the hustle to get where I wanted to be. It uplifted me, taught me to strive for greatness, and dream big! These principles hold true for me in 2010 as they did back in the day.

In this book, I take some of the hottest hip-hop songs ever made and put a spin on the titles to show how those words helped to shape my past and my future. I hope this book will inspire other young women and men to learn the game the DAS way and to understand how to climb the ladder of success on their own terms!

PressReset.me Publishing

ISBN
978-0-615-3847-9

$19.95
www.thehiphopprofessional.com   www.pressreset.me

# TABLE OF CONTENTS

Kendall B. and Shanti at Z89 Radio Station (SU)

Tisha Cambell-Martin and Shanti Das, '92 People's Choice Awards

# CHAPTER ONE
## "CAN'T KNOCK THE HUSTLE"
### (Hard Work Really Does Pay Off!)

Jay-Z definitely got his hustle on, and so did I. I've been working since I was 13, selling candy in middle school, working at an ice cream parlor in the 9th grade, at Six Flags in the 10th grade, serving as a security guard in the 11th grade, and telemarketing in the 12th grade. Once I realized my passion was music, I was a beast, and I wouldn't stop until I got a job in the business. Like Soulja Boy said, "We gotta hop up out that bed and turn our Swag on!"

I got up every day, put a smile on my face, and knew I had to "Make It Happen," just as Kevin Liles did! When I was at B.E. Mays High School, I used to go up to V-103 radio station in Atlanta and volunteer with Ray Boyd (then Program Director). I knew it would be a great starting point for me to get into music.

Although I got my start back in the early 90s, some of the same principles still apply. By the time I was in college at Syracuse University (SU), where I majored in television, radio, and film at the S.I. Newhouse School of Public Communications, everyone thought I already had a full-time position in the game. It was like Eve's hit "Who's That Girl?" I was at every necessary function I could attend. You have to be aggressive and learn to get involved in many activities relative to your area of interest. At SU, I was an on-air disc jockey, promotions director at the campus radio station Z-89, and a staff music writer for the campus newsletter. I also attended various hip-hop and music industry conferences and networked with as many

2

folks, who were already in the music business, as I could (shout-out to the Judy Lane crew—JD, Tina, Skeeter Rock, Pat, Chantel, and Christi).

Some of the conferences/events included Jack the Rapper (thanks to Mike Mauldin for getting me a pass), NBPC, BRE, Impact (Def Jam Saturday night party), Sprite Soul Train Pre-Show, Million Dollar Music Conference, and the Hip-Hop Cultural Initiative at Howard University, where I landed my first radio drop from 2Pac for my radio show, and where I first met Diddy (he was known as Puff Daddy back then, and I still call him Puffy). These were all good people to know and learn from and good people to help me get to where I wanted to go.

By the time the summer of my sophomore year rolled around, I landed a job at Capitol Records as a Promotions Assistant to Keith Frye, the Vice President of Urban Promotions. I hustled all summer, doing everything asked of me, and then some. Next summer, Dee Dee Murray, the young woman I was filling in for, returned from maternity leave, but they still asked me back because of the job I had done the previous summer (shout-out to Tisha Campbell-Martin and Mona for allowing me to work with them and assist on Tisha's promo run).

It's funny, while at Capitol, I realized that the offices for LaFace Records were upstairs from our office. Instead of coffee breaks, I took "LaFace" breaks. I tried to take advantage of every moment possible. I used to go up and hang with Sharliss Asbury and Lamont Boles, and they would give me guidance/insight into the biz. They were about to release the "Boomerang" soundtrack, which went on to become a huge hit. I knew that's where I wanted to be.

3

I was well on my way to making my mark in the business because I worked extremely hard, was committed to succeeding, and did not take any of those opportunities for granted. I held myself accountable and let my work speak for itself. You don't have to front when you have the quality work to show for it. And I did all this while carrying myself like a lady and respecting myself, which is essential in a male-dominated industry. That's what it takes. That's the choice we have to make to stay on the right path.

**SO, LADIES, AS BUSTA RHYMES SAID, "WHAT'S IT GONNA BE?"**

Maria (Sister) and Shanti - SU Graduation

Dorm Shot at SU

Shanti and MC Lyte

# CHAPTER TWO
## "I CRAM TO UNDERSTAND"
### (Why Go to College?)

MC Lyte "crammed to understand" and that's exactly how I felt about studying. Why did I need to stay in school and finish, since I was so intent on being successful in this business? After all, there weren't many classes being offered about the music industry in college—none leading to a career at least. You might also wonder, "Why stay in school or why get a master's degree?" Yet the one thing I learned about this business, especially now, is that you always need to have something to fall back on. That's what a college degree can do for you. Never underestimate that fact.

I saw that Syracuse had strong media programs in areas of interest to me, including communications (television and radio), so if the music thing didn't work out, I would have some sort of formal training to fall back on. There was also a ton of activities to get involved in on campus, which provided a great training ground. For example, they had a small campus radio station. Seeing another opportunity to hone my skills, I eventually wound up with my own hip-hop radio show on Z-89. They also had newsletters, newspapers, TV stations, and more. These were other avenues of potential employment to explore, just in case.

Record labels today aren't offering the lucrative employee contracts as they did 10 years ago. I have seen so many people, who really couldn't transfer their music skills into other lucrative careers, laid off from record companies. Once their moment was over, it was over

for good. But I wasn't going to be another casualty of fleeting fame. I had a backup plan. In fact, I had a few of them, and so should anyone starting out, especially if you're a woman.

Another plus to being in college is that most major labels, TV stations, radio stations, and entertainment publications offer summer internships only for college students. You won't be paid, but you receive credit. Interning is highly recommended because it allows you to see if that is the job, company, or industry that you like. You get to make contacts and experience hands-on training. Many companies go on to hire past interns. And if nothing more, it gets your foot in the door!

Today, more and more colleges have hip-hop and music industry courses as a part of their curriculum. Syracuse University, for example, has the Bandier Music Program, a multi-disciplinary degree that includes an understanding of music, communications, marketing, and other aspects of promoting talent. I sit on the advisory board of the Bandier Program and the Newhouse School, and we have many alumni in the business who return to speak to the students regularly and provide a wealth of knowledge and information about the music industry.

For successful women with years of experience in the entertainment business, it's also a great idea to participate in continuing education classes. Major labels are run just like any other corporation. Music might be an art form, but it's still about the bottom line—selling product. You need to bring it and build a strong set of business and management skills. Some labels even pay for continuing education classes. I participated in one outstanding course at Harvard University called "Effective Strategies for Media Companies."

It provided me with an in-depth understanding of how other big companies in media entertainment succeed (Apple, Microsoft, and so on). I was able to bring back the best practices I learned at Harvard to my record label, giving me a professional edge that did not go unnoticed by the higher-ups.

**REMEMBER, PEOPLE WILL RESPECT YOU EVEN MORE WHEN YOU TAKE THE INITIATIVE AND BUILD UP YOUR OWN BASE OF KNOWLEDGE. LADIES HANDLE YOUR B-I!**

Keith Frye and Shanti

# CHAPTER THREE
## "HOW DO YOU WANT IT?"
(Getting In and Staying In!)

Remember that 2Pac joint, "How Do You Want It?" Well, once I had a good taste of working at Capitol Records that summer, I knew I wanted in, and I had to figure out a way to stay in. I wanted to work in hip-hop so bad, and I was determined to land a permanent job after college.

I remember going up to Russell Simmons in the lobby at a Jack the Rapper convention one day and saying, "You don't know me, but by the end of this conference, you will!"

I told him that I was trying to work my way into the business, and I was there to network and meet other execs. He looked at me, smiled, and just said, "Okay." I knew he was skeptical. He's probably heard stuff like that from eager young kids a million times. But I couldn't be afraid to network, ask questions, and put myself out there to express my desire for a job.

After several days of "working" the lobby and being a "Soldier" like Erykah Badu, I was unstoppable! I introduced myself to all the execs, attended many panels, and I wasn't afraid to ask questions about anything and everything. I got the answers I needed. At the end of the seminar, I ran back into Russell. He stood right in front of me, and he said, "I saw you out there doing your thing!" I felt as if I had just won the Lotto!

He probably doesn't remember that comment now, but at the time, it was a big boost of encouragement. Russell Simmons saw me on my grind and, if only for a brief moment, acknowledged my hard work and determination. That conversation not only magnified how much I wanted to succeed, it showed me that I could, and I would.

I remember my mentor Mel Smith inviting me to an Uptown Records event in New York. I knew this would be a great spot for me to network with some music execs. Of course, I was still a student—a *broke* college student—but I had to find a way to make it happen. I scrounged up enough money to buy a roundtrip Greyhound bus ticket to the city. The drive from Syracuse to New York is normally three hours and some change. Well, by bus, it was more than six hours. But I didn't care. I had to be at that event. So, I went down to the city and made some great connections. I slept four hours on Mel's hotel **floor** until my 6 a.m. bus and headed back to Syracuse for afternoon class. That's what it takes.

Yet, more encounters with people in the industry I admired were helping to stoke the fires of my ambition. When I first met Puffy, he was making things happen at Uptown Records. It took a while to get an appointment, and even then, he left me in the waiting room for more than an hour before seeing me. When I did, he didn't have anything for me, but he did offer encouragement. And I took it. I saw what his hard work could achieve and resolved to be just as much of a beast. Soon after, I took an internship with Sony, and that was just the beginning. I was hellbent on moving up.

No one is going to give you anything in this business. You have to speak up and let people know what your dreams and ambitions are. As they say in the Sprite commercials, "Obey your thirst." Well, I

had a thirst to make my dreams a reality.

Like Boss, I was getting "Deeper" into this music game. I went on to work at Capitol for two summers, after which I graduated from Syracuse University and began interning at Sony Music. Four months later, Keith Frye, the same man who hired me at Capitol, called me and said he was now consulting for LaFace Records. Antonio "LA" Reid and Babyface had recently set up shop back in my hometown of Atlanta. Because Keith saw how dedicated I was to my craft, he recommended me for a newly created position at LaFace. I interviewed with Scott Folks and LA Reid, and the rest was history. Four months out of college, I was hired as Promotions Director, making $30,000 a year. I hit the road the next two years with OutKast, Toni Braxton, Usher, TLC, and Goodie Mob. It was happening. My dreams were becoming reality. I was quenching that thirst.

**CARPE DIEM, LADIES—ALWAYS SEIZE THE MOMENT!**

Poon Daddy, Big Boi, Andre 3000, Blue Williams, Chris Lova Lova (aka Ludacris) and Shanti

Shanti chillin' in the S.W.A.T.S.

Goodie Mob, The Notorious B.I.G., Lil' Cease, Bernard Parks & Shanti

# CHAPTER FOUR
## "WHATTA MAN"
### (You Never Know Where Your Blessings Will Come From.)

n the words of the great female rap duo Salt-n-Pepa, "Whatta man whatta man, whatta mighty, mighty good man… yes, he is!" Contrary to what some might say, there are some great men in hip-hop and the music industry. I was surprised by how many men (and not as many women) supported me throughout my career and showed me the utmost respect. You can earn that respect by demonstrating that you respect yourself. As long as you carry yourself in a manner that does your mama and daddy proud, you will not have as many problems working in this business.

One thing I did early on was to wear baggy jeans, sneakers, and hats all the time. It was my uniform. I was chillin' like one of the boys. A friend of mine gave me the nickname "Shoestring" so that I could have a handle. I quickly had many male friends as mentors, and they treated me like their little sister. That worked well for me. It diverted the attention away from me as a sexual object. It protected me from the advances of certain players who you sometimes have to deal with in any industry, but particularly in hip-hop. These guys knew me for my mind and spirit, and not my body, and that was just how I wanted it.

My first male mentor was Ray Boyd, whom I mentioned earlier. He was the Program Director at Atlanta's V-103 radio station. Ray also knew Keith Frye, my boss at Capitol Records, who became a mentor and like a father to me. They both guided me early on, teaching

me the ropes of the game. My next great mentor would be Antonio "LA" Reid.

A funny story about LA—while still in college, I went to Washington, DC to visit a girlfriend and attend the Budweiser Superfest concert. I was at the airport in baggage claim, and it was so crowded, I couldn't see my luggage coming around on the carousel. I'm so little that, once I saw my bags, I couldn't reach them, so I tapped this guy on the shoulder and said, "Scuse me, can you get my bags for me right there?" He looked at me for a long second, saw I was serious, and proceeded to get both my bags, as a gentleman should. I thanked him and went to the pay phone (we didn't have cellies back then) to call my friend. About 10 minutes later, I saw this same guy walking down the airport with all this Louis Vuitton luggage and what looked like five or six skycaps. It looked like something out of a scene from *Coming to America*. By the time he got to the door, I realized who he was, and my mouth dropped. It was hit-maker Antonio "LA" Reid! Little did I know at the time that the dude I was telling to get my bags would be the same guy to give me my first big break.

So, I definitely have experienced some "mighty good" men in this business, and I have had lasting working relationships with many of them. As an act of respect and admiration, here's a super shout-out to my male mentors and those who inspired and helped me along the way: Ray Boyd, Keith Frye, Wayne K. Brown, Antonio "LA" Reid, Babyface, Dorsey James, Lamont Boles, Donnie Ienner, Jermaine Dupri, Jam Master J (R.I.P.), Kay Gee, Mike Mauldin, Diddy, Steve Rifkind, Kevin Liles, Jay Brown, Danny Meiseles, Mel Smith, Marvin McIntyre, Eric Nicks, "Big Jon" Platt, Sincere Thompson, Mark Shimmel, Mark Pitts, Steve Stoute, James Andrews, Donald Woodard, Ed Lover, Chaka Zulu, Derek Jackson, Greg Street,

Shakir Stewart (R.I.P.) Tony Mercedes, Al Manerson, Shakim, DJ Eddie F, Stephen Hill, Ryan Cameron, Rob Stone, Kendall B., Chuck Bone, George Daniels, Charles Dixon, Devyne Stephens, Ryan Glover, Kenny Burns, Doug Davis, Blue Williams, Chad Elliott, FUT, D-Nice, Sway, Funkmaster Flex, Big Boi and Rico Wade.

**AS HEAVY D AND THE BOYZ SAID, I GOT "NUTTIN' BUT LOVE" FOR YA GUYS—THANKS SO MUCH!**

Shanti's LAFACE photo shoot

# CHAPTER FIVE
## "GIT UP, GIT OUT?"
### (Gettin' the Tough Job Done)

The first big hip-hop act I ever worked with was Outkast back in '93. They told us we all had to "Git Up, Git Out and Git Something!" I took those words to heart.

I worked my way up from Promotions Director to Senior Director of Marketing at LaFace. I dedicated myself 24/7 to accomplish my goals. Literally. I worked in the office by day, took dinner/drink meetings after work, was in the clubs distributing promo material or covering performances by night (I did every hole in the wall club performance imaginable with Usher and Outkast - across many states), rode in the bottom bunk on the bus (lol) with TLC for the CRAZYSEXYCOOL tour, and finally I would end up in the studio by the wee hours of the morning. There was no time to sleep, I had to get it in!!

As women, we have to work extra hard to show our commitment and passion to our job. We aren't always invited to the cigar rooms, strip clubs, or, in mainstream corporate America, the golf courses. Consequently, we miss some networking opportunities available to men. That's why I created my own opportunities. I figured out how to finagle my way into that man's world when I started working with Outkast.

Now, I knew that Outkast and most of the local DJs in Atlanta loved their strip clubs. So, I threw a DJ Appreciation Party at the Gentleman's Club, the hottest strip club in town back then. Although it wasn't my first choice to be there, I knew I had to break Outkast and do unconventional things to get them the right attention from the right people and promote their music. I made it a point not to drink while I was there. But I also made sure my DJs were happy and got our music played. I found myself a corner to chill in while they enjoyed the party. I accomplished my goals that night, all the while demanding respect and letting folks know I was there to carry out a job, *and that was it*.

A few months later, I was promoting Outkast in Los Angeles. I went out with some friends that night to a club to see Ice Cube perform. I was hanging with some of my folks from 92.3 The Beat to schmooze them—part of the job when you're a promotions director—and we were all kickin' it at the show. At one point, some guy just upped and grabbed my behind! I turned to look but couldn't see who did it. Then, it happened again! I felt so violated. But the third time, I was ready like Public Enemy to "shut 'em down." As soon as he pulled his hand back, I caught a glimpse of who did it. I swung on him like Ali during the Frazier fight (tiny me and big him). Little did I know he was from one of the worst gangs in L.A. He was taking aim to swing back at me, and my friends swooped me up and carried me out on their backs. But not before I landed my punch dead in his chest!

To this day, my good friend "Big Jon" Platt jokes about that night. I don't condone fighting, but we, as women, have to protect ourselves from the B.S. we sometimes face in the game.

In this business, there are times when you might be put in an uncomfortable situation, but you have to stay focused and do things the right way. Although I do not recommend stripping as a profession, I knew I had to get this party done for Outkast, and I couldn't be afraid to go in those clubs. I had to play my position as a promotions director and be around my male counterparts. But outside the job, I always had to create a balance for myself, by paying it forward and talking to young women about other business opportunities in music. I feel it's part of my responsibility to show them a different way.

As women, it's important that we help each other and let those who come after us know that there are many other professional options. So many girls only see the videos and the stereotypical roles of women depicted in that imagery. It's up to the women already in the game to provide knowledge and insight and set examples for the aspiring female generation. It's difficult as a woman working in a business that sometimes degrades other women. On the one hand, I am not for censorship, and I believe in freedom of speech. On the other hand, some artists take it too far. So, we have to do our part in the community to speak on empowerment panels, mentor (shout-out to Essence magazine for their panels, Susan Taylor and the National Cares Mentoring Movement, Michael Baisden's "One Million Mentors Campaign," Steve Harvey's Mentoring Weekend, Mary J Blige/Steve Stoute's organization FFAWN), and be better role models for our young women and men on the come-up. Many artists have wonderful foundations that do great work in communities around the world.

I grew up listening to lyrics that used profanity and the B-word. It wasn't as bad for me because I had a stable upbringing, and my mother instilled good values in our family. She taught us to have high self-esteem and respect for others.

We knew not to repeat any of those words or to call anyone out of their names. So, for me, the music really was art. I loved the beats, and I took it as pure entertainment. Today, it's much harder for young girls to make that distinction. In this reality show culture, where every little moment is put up on YouTube, life imitates art more than ever.

That's why you've got to learn to differentiate. Don't get lost in this crazy world. You get in and plan for life after the business. You don't define yourself by this stuff, either. It's OK to be "in" the business, but you don't have to be "of" the business. Just do what it takes to get the job done, all the while keeping your reputation and your integrity intact.

**LADIES, AS NAS ONCE SAID, "I KNOW I CAN, BE WHAT I WANNA BE, IF I WORK HARD AT IT, I'LL BE WHERE I WANNA BE!"**

Shanti and Chilli of TLC

DL Warfield, T-Boz of TLC and Shanti

# CHAPTER SIX
## "HOW LOW CAN YOU GO? HOW LOW CAN YOU GO?"
(So U *Think* U Wanna Be a Video Chick?)

Ludacris recently gave us a smash hit with "How Low Can You Go?" Love the song, but I wanna put a different spin on it. This chapter will ask you, "How **high** can you go? How **high** can you go?"

There are **many** other professional opportunities for women in music/entertainment. Prepare yourselves. This section will be longer than the others are, but it's important for me to list the various career paths and executives, **past and present**.

Ladies, there are many grand possibilities out there for you. You should shoot for the moon and the stars. Aside from aspiring to be a rapper, singer, or video vixen, you can become:

• An Award-Winning Entertainment Executive such as Suzanne De Passe or the first African-American woman to ever get hired as the Chairman of a major label such as Sylvia Rhone

• President of a TV network such as Debra Lee of BET, or President of a major label/group/production company such as Michele Anthony, Julie Greenwald, Sharon Heyward, Polly Anthony, Jean Riggins, and Tracey Edmonds

• A Rapper, Actor, Producer, Cover Girl, and Business Mogul such as Queen Latifah or a Rapper, Icon/Entrepreneur such as MC Lyte

• Owner of a radio chain/TV outlet such as Cathy Hughes from Radio One

• A VH1/MTV Television Executive such as Christina Norman (President of MTV, now CEO of OWN), Angela Fisher, or Whitney Gayle-Benta
• Owner of a magazine/Website such as Jamie Foster Brown, Editor-in-Chief such as Gayle King, Danyel Smith and Angela Burt-Murray, and Entertainment Editor such as Cori Murray
• A General Manager such as Kirdis Postelle, Hannah Kang, Dedra Tate, and Lisa Ellis; a booking agent such as Cara Lewis; or COO of DTP such as Aiyisha Obafemi
• An Artist Manager such as Mona Scott-Young, Phillana Williams, Jonnetta Patton, Tina Douglas, Tina Davis, Constance Schwartz, Barkue Tubman, Claudine Joseph, Hillary Weston, Toya Hankins and Laurie Dobbins
• A top Choreographer such as Fatima Robinson, Jamaica Craft, Laurie-Ann Gibson, Tanisha Scott, and Nefertiti
• An Entertainment Attorney such as Moraima Ivory, Denise Brown, Louise West, Wendy Credle, Nova Perry, Jill Ramsey, Joy Warren, Monica Ewing, Sandra Brown, Phaedra Parks, and Angela Rogers
• A top Clothing Stylist such as June Ambrose, Rachel Johnson, Marni Senafonte, Andrea Lieberman, Misa Hylton-Brim, Sybil Pennix, Calyann, Monica Morrow, Crystal Streets, and Tameka Raymond; a top hair stylist to the stars such as Tippi Shorter, Marie Brown, Lisa Pope, Ursula Stephen, and Carla Bone; or a top makeup artist such as Ashunta Sheriff, Yolanda Frederick, and Mylah
• A Music Publisher such as Jody Gerson, Ethiopia Habtemariam, Catherine Brewton, Jessica Rivera, and Shante Paige
• Owner of an Image Agency such as Brandi Simpkins, Carline Balan, and Krystal Thorpe; or a Video Producer such as Nomi Roher
• A Media Publicist such as Patti Webster, Yvette Noel-Schure, Marvet Britto, Amanda Silverman, Gwendolyn Quinn, Tammy Warren, Phylicia Fant, Shante Bacon, Saptosa Foster, Tracy Nguyen,

Sabrina Thompson, Margeaux Watson, Jana Fleishman, Lorraine Robertson, Tammy Brook, Chanel Green, LaVerne Perry-Kennedy, Vickie Charles, Syreta Oglesby, Aliya Crawford, Michelle Huff, Christina Rice, Chrissy Murray, Tresa Sanders, April Love, Leslie Short, Shirronda Sweet-Tafari and Paula Witt

- A Marketing Executive such as Karen Mason, Ashley Fox, Sheila Coates, Suzanne Burge-Taylor, Jackie Rhinehart, Ashaunna Ayars, Davett Singletary, Capricorn, Tatia Adams Fox, Jill Capone, Cameo Carlson, Lisa Cambridge-Mitchell, Joi Pitts, Katina Bynum, Leota Blacknor, Shari Bryant, Chaka Pilgrim, Elise Wright, Tracy Waples, Meda Leacock, Liz Hausle, Quincy Jackson, Amber Noble, Lesvia Castro, Joanne Madhere, Melantha Hodge, Caron Veazy, Gita Williams, Kimberly Mason, Marsha St Hubert, Vanessa Levy, Michelle Murray, Bianca Moore, Carolyn Williams, Terri Haskins, Dana Hill and Lynn Scott
- A blogger such as Necole Bitchie, Natasha Eubanks, Angel, CJ, Janee, MissInfo, Hillary Crosley, Clutch, & Sandra Rose. Editor-at-Large for Bet.com such as Kim Orsorio
- A Brand Strategist such as Lori Lambert, Marilyn Batchelor, Sheri Riley, Lauren Wirtzer, Kim Cooper King, Aria Wright, Dolly Turner, Camille Hackney, Devronya Brathwaite, Kobi Wu, and CeCe Smooth
- VP of Music/Ent for Bet.com such as Rhonda Cowan
- Video Production Executive such as Gina Harrell, Robin Simms, Gabby Peluso, and Michelle Montgomery
- A top party planner/event promoter such as Jessica Rosenblum, Keisha Walker, Tammy Ford, and Toi Crawford; or a Creative Show Director such as Kim Burse
- An author such as Dream Hampton, Lyah Beth Leflore, Sil Lai Abrams, or Thembisa Mshaka (also a copywriter); or a Writer such as Gail Mitchell & Sonia Murray

- Head of Operations for Rowdy Entertainment such as Sharliss Asbury
- Senior VP of Development/Production of FoxxKing such as Laronda Sutton or a top retail buyer such as Violet Brown
- Talent consultant like Melanie Lewis Massey
- Legal analyst, TV host, lawyer, and vocalist such as Lauren Lake (WEEN co-founder)
- Executive Director of the Hip-Hop Summit Action Network turned director of public affairs for the International Trade Administration of President Barack Obama such as Valeisha Butterfield (WEEN co-founder)
- TV personality such as Rosci, Alesha Renee, La La Vazquez, Free, Bevy Smith, Egypt, and Amanda Diva (blogger/poet)
- A Radio On-air Personality such as Angie Martinez, Wendy Williams, Miss Jones, Big Lez, Rashan Ali, Ramona DeBreaux, Mami Chula, Carol Blackmon, Helen Little, Cha Cha, Cherry Martinez, Magic, Angela Yee and Eboni Elektra
- A&R Executive such as Karen Kwak, Candy Tookes, Gwen Miles, Vida Sparks, Wendy Day, Dee Dee Murray, Angelique Miles, Celeste Moses, and Azar Shahsavarani Bogan
- Artist Development reps such as Dyana Williams, Sheila Eldridge, and Ivory Weems
- Vice Presidents and National Radio Promotions Executives such as Martha Thomas-Frye, Johnnie Walker (founder of NABFEME and Women Who Jam), Daria Langford, Kathi Moore, Traci Adams, Colleen Wilson, Michelle Madison, Juliette Jones, Nicole Sellers, Sam Selolwane, P.J. Jones, Tyesh Harris, Mona Lisa, Charita Brittenum and Cannon Kent
- Execs for the Recording Academy such as Elizabeth Healy, Michelle Rhea Caplinger, Lisa Zahn, and Erin Baxter

- A DJ such as DJ Kiss, Beverly Bond, and Traci Steele
Photographer like Donna Permell and Ashley Reid
- Tour marketing rep such as Kira Daniels and Tanya Baysmore
- A Rap Editor like Shannita Williams
- Head of Creative at a label such as Sandra Brummels and
Denise Williams
- A Digital/Mobile business development consultant such as Jamilah Barnes Creekmur or an international marketer such as Vivian Scott-Chew
- Executive Assistant to a music mogul such as Karleen Roy,
Sandie Smith, Joshlyn Hargrove, Catherine Ahn, Janice Faison, Beth
Hawkins and Marie Maullon

## LADIES, AS 112 SAID, "THE SKY IS THE LIMIT!" THERE IS SO MUCH MORE TO HIP-HOP AND THE MUSIC BUSINESS THAN MEETS THE EYE, IF YOU KNOW WHAT I MEAN!

Monica and Shanti

Shanti and Johnnie Walker

Left Eye of TLC and Shanti

# CHAPTER SEVEN
## "BEAUTIFUL SKIN"
(Love the Skin You're In!)


The Goodie Mob told us to respect ourselves as women and to love ourselves. Oil of Olay commercials told us to "love the skin you're in." This holds as true today for me as it did when I first heard those words, and it should for you.

I never tried to be someone I was not in the business. One way I survived the game was by holding true to who I was morally and spiritually and by staying loyal to my oldest and dearest "friends" (how many of us have them?)—many of whom were from elementary & middle school. I am not claiming a "holier than thou" mentality, but I did try to stay true to my roots. I came into the industry as a country girl from Atlanta, and I am still that same girl 20 years later.

Many of us get into the business and find the need to act or look like who we think are the stars. What is really needed is to "keep it 100." I mean, there's nothing wrong with getting your glam on—getting a weave or a little "work" done is fine. But do it for yourself, not to please others. As Mary J Blige says, "Take me as I am!"

Beauty comes in all shapes and sizes. We should not measure beauty by only the women we see in the videos or on the red carpet. It's like the Dove self-esteem campaign says, *"young women have to learn to be more confident about themselves."* I never put any of my sisters down because of how they did or didn't look. It never mattered what they had or didn't have. Who are we to define what might be

beautiful to others? What I found out early on was to stay away from the drama, mind my own business, and treat everyone with the same amount of respect.

I never wanted to gossip because the name that my dad gave me (Shanti) comes from Indian decent meaning *peace*... so I try to live by that definition. I just wanted to keep my relationships solid because you never knew whom you needed to ask a favor of, or whom you might be reporting to one day. We live in an ever-changing business, and you should never burn bridges out of pettiness or disrespect. It only clouds your judgment and creates a bad rep.

We, as women, should not degrade one another. Instead, we have to learn to uplift each other and remember, "All Hail the Covergirl Queen—Ladies **First**!" Shout-out to Monie Love and Queen Latifah! We have to learn to check our brothers who disrespect us and to teach them to love us in a way we would be proud of. Let's set examples for the young ones coming behind us. It's not corny to be your own person and not follow the crowd. Be secure in who you are, and like Rakim said, "Know the Ledge!"

Don't be afraid also to share a contact or pass along a résumé. Women get too territorial in this game. We can all help each other. No one succeeds entirely on her own. If you truly love yourself and have high self-esteem, you will have no problem staying the course and lending a helping hand along the way. Latifah told us to have U.N.I.T.Y. years ago. "Who you callin' a b*tch or ho?" If we spent half as much time doing our job and trying to help each other as we spend knocking one another down, we'd be much better positioned in the hierarchy of this business.

31

# SO, LADIES, DON'T HATE... CELEBRATE! AND CONGRATULATE!

RUN DMC and Shanti

Busta Ako[...]

Shanti and Puffy/Diddy/Puff Daddy

Jeff Dixon, Shanti and Chaka Zulu

# CHAPTER EIGHT
## "IT'S NOT ALL ABOUT THE BENJAMINS"
### (I'm Not Out for Only "Dead Presidents" to Represent Me!)

Puff Daddy & The Family gave us a smash hit with "All About the Benjamins." There's a lot to be learned from those words. One important lesson is to look at the converse of that title. Sometimes, it's NOT all about the Benjamins, and C.ash doesn't R.ule E.verything A.round M.e.

As a music industry veteran, when I look to hire that next hot executive, I want the person not driven by his or her paycheck, but by passion! Puff Daddy is one of the most driven and passionate people I know in hip-hop. And anyone looking to make it big has to have that same drive. Everyone wants and needs people on his or her team who absolutely love what they do, no matter how unglamorous it might seem.

You have to remember, you're still in the business, which is a privilege. Do you even know how many people want your spot? In this game, you snooze; you lose! But you'll keep stepping up as long as you stick with it and do the right thing. You might need to intern for free but be the best intern around. If you are charged with faxing getting coffee, going across the Brooklyn Bridge to get cheesecake or answering phones, you had better work your butt off to make yourself shine above all the rest. Those who handle pressure with grace and professionalism stand out from the crowd of those who want it all ASAP and have this warped sense of entitlement. So many are misled by the overnight success stories and reality TV stars. No one is going to give you anything; you have to **earn** your place in greatness. You can be "all you can be" just like they say in the Army ads In this game, you also have to be willing to make sacrifices. The

entertainment industry doesn't have regular nine-to-five jobs. Our hours are ten-to-seven, and then some. You get in later, but you also work **much** later. Seven o'clock is actually not realistic. I used to leave work around eight or nine every night. Then, there are the dinners, shows, artist release parties, an so on. When I first got into the business, I put off having a family to pursue my career. Although some women have successfully found a way to balance having a family and working in the business, most waited years to get married and have a child, got divorced, or stayed single.

If you are like me, you are trying to focus on your personal life 20 years after the fact. If you want to climb this ladder of success, you have to remain hungry and be willing to put in the work. With fewer jobs than ever and with the decline in music sales, it's extremely difficult to have a career and a life.

Only the best of the best will rise to the top. You have to be there and be accountable. People have to know you'll follow through and complete the task. I took care of every little detail for my artists, however small. They knew they could rely on me for anything, and the greatest compliment to me was gaining their respect. I reached the top of my marketing career by becoming the executive vice president of marketing, having overseen the careers of Outkast, Goodie Mob, Usher, Busta Rhymes, Jermaine Dupri, TLC, Akon, Erykah Badu, Lil' Bow Wow, Ashanti, Run DMC, and many more. I was also one of the first people to want to sign Ludacris. I knew him when he worked at the radio station as "Chris Lova Lova." I used to hang out with him and his manager Chaka Zulu during their on-air shift. Chris saw how hard I worked on 'Kast and Goodie Mob and wanted to be down with us. I brought him to LaFace and negotiated for months, but we dropped the ball on that one and let another label sign him. Of course, Ludacris has gone on to become a massive superstar. Luda, Chaka Zulu, and Jeff have built an incredible empire.

Hats off to them! That was a huge letdown for me, but I did not let it keep me down. I continued to let my passion show in my work, which gave me a great reputation in the business. Don't let money be your driving force. The paper will come. Be creative, think out of the box, and **love** what you do, even if it's just the grunt work that needs to get done while you put in your time. As Ford Motor Company says, "Quality is job one!"

## C'MON LADIES! "TIME TO MAKE THE DOUGHNUTS!"

Shanti and Sylvia Rhone at R&B Live NYC

# CHAPTER NINE
## "THE POWER OF THE P"
(Not Exactly What You Think!)

R. Kelly and Jay-Z talked about the "Power of the P." But I want to talk about the **three** P's: Perseverance, Professionalism, and Positioning.

**Perseverance:** You have to be in it for the long haul. It took me almost 15 years to become an Executive Vice President. It might not take you as long, but you have to have goals based on realistic expectations, and you have to stay focused.

There will always be people who obtain success quicker than others do in the music industry, but those who take their time to learn the game and perfect their craft end up having the most staying power. Success isn't a perfect upward trajectory. There are always going to be difficulties on your career path. It's how you deal with those downs and see past them that will determine your longevity in this business.

For example, when I quit my post at Arista Records almost a decade ago, I went home for a few months and was depressed. I eventually snapped out of it and decided not to give up on the business. I knew there must be a better situation out there for me. The reason why I left Arista had nothing to do with LA Reid; I had a few issues with my direct report. So, I networked at home and ran into my good friend Jermaine Dupri. JD had a label deal through Sony Music at the time, and he convinced me to come back to New York and interview with

then Chairman of Columbia Records, Donnie Ienner. I interviewed and was hired as Vice President of Urban Marketing—the title I'd been longing for. Six months later, I was made head of the department. So, ladies, don't ever give up. Stay the course on what you want and build relationships. As Anthony Williams would say on *Project Runway,* "Keep yo eye on the priiiize!"

But when you have built those strong relationships and call in favors from friends/colleagues, be strategic about the "ask." You have to respect the fact that these are very important people with incredibly busy schedules. You only ask for favors, when you really and truly need the help.

**Professionalism:** I know we all fall a little behind sometimes, but I cannot stress enough the importance of returning phone calls and replying to e-mails. People appreciate the common courtesy of a response. Proper follow-through goes a long way in this business or any business, for that matter. We live in a hi-tech society now, and there are multiple ways to get back to someone—a cell phone call, e-mail, text, voicemail, tweet, Facebook message—there's no excuse. Yes, it can be overwhelming sometimes. On a typical day, you might have hundreds of e-mail messages flowing into your inbox, and not every piece of correspondence is as urgent as the next. One thing that worked for me was to ask my intern or assistant to call folks back if I didn't have the time to deal with their queries directly. At least there was some level of correspondence. Everyone deserves acknowledgement. I traveled all the time and was often too busy to stop for even a minute, but I knew the importance of maintaining communication, and it made my job a lot easier when I needed to get certain people on the phone. Because I respected others, they gave me that same respect in turn. Again, it comes down to being accountable.

People get to know you as the person who follows through. That's a rare thing in this business, but it's also a way you can stand out from the crowd.

**Positioning:** Sometimes it really *is* just a matter of being in the right place at the right time. You never know who you're going to meet (or where), so always be strategic about where you go, whom you sit next to at dinners and luncheons, and which clients you take to certain events. Chris Lighty (Violator mgmt) always showed up with a purpose and worked the room strategically. I also learned a great deal about succeeding in hip-hop from the way Russell Simmons, Lyor Cohen, Kevin Liles, Julie Greenwald, and Mike Kyser built Def Jam. They moved like a team and *always* positioned every move they made to a tee.

## CHECKMATE, LADIES! WHAT'S *YOUR* NEXT MOVE?

Andre 3000, Big Boi and Shanti at the Source Awards

Greg Street, Dee Dee Murray and Shanti

# CHAPTER TEN
## "AIN'T NO HALF-STEPPIN"
### (WARNING: Slackers Not Allowed!)

Big Daddy Kane once said, "for you to beat me, it's gonna take a miracle." You have to treat each job opportunity as if you're going to war—but be strategic in how you fight. As Sun Tzu says, "every battle is won before it's ever fought."

Back when I was working hard to break Outkast, I wouldn't take no for an answer. Many people told us that they were too "country" and could not rap. They received a lot of early love from certain cities, such as Atlanta (all DJs there), the San Francisco Bay Area (thanks, Sway & Tech), Dallas (thanks, Greg Street), and Chicago (thanks, and R.I.P., Pinkhouse). But not New York. That was the hardest market for us to crack. I wasn't going to stop, though—not until they had the respect they deserved.

We booked shows all over town (shout-out to Maria Davis/Mad-Wednesdays and Grandma Funk/The Funk Hut), hired street team King (as he was known at the time) Sincere Thompson of Frontline Marketing, and worked DJs Clue, Big Kap, Kay Slay, Enuff, Clark Kent, and Funkmaster Flex—we worked 'em **hard**! And we got our dear friend Puff Daddy on board. LA Reid and I pulled out all stops to get this group exposed in the Tri-State area. Finally, after weeks and months of mortal combat, we began to saturate the New York market, and people started noddin' their heads to the sounds of Outkast.

It all culminated with the Source awards. Outkast won big as "Best New Rap Group" in 1995. It was just the three of us—Big Boi, Andre 3000, and I—and the **East/West** coast were **Deep** in the building! They accepted the award and Dre uttered those infamous words "the **South** got somethin' to say!"

Just because you are from a different city or rep a certain town doesn't mean you can't fulfill your dreams and get people to buy into your product, idea, or plan. Like LL Cool J, you have to keep "doin' it and doin' it and doin' it well!" It doesn't matter what disadvantages you might think you have. With persistence, your passion and talent will shine through, and you'll see your payoff. At the end of the day, people love to see the underdog win. First, you have to tough it out and work, work, work. No excuses!

**LADIES, THERE IS NO HALF-STEPPIN' IN THIS GAME. YOU GOTTA "SH\*T OR GET OFF THE POT," AS MY MAMA USED TO SAY!**

JD, Shanti and Usher

Shanti at the
'94 Southernplayalistic Cookout

Donell Jones, Shanti & Barkue Tubman

# CHAPTER ELEVEN
## "LOST ONES"
(Stay Ahead of the Game!)

Hip-Hop Goddess Lauryn Hill once told us, "Everything you did has already been done." Well, that might be true, but only some of the time. It's still important to think out of the box and figure out how to flip old ideas into fresh ones. You have to find the courage to go where few folks have gone before and take the time to think of something new. Apple said it best, "Think Different!"

Puff Daddy was a beast back in the early '90s and always kept it F-R-E-S-H! I remember when he came out with the idea to market the Notorious B.I.G. and Craig Mack together. He literally packaged their promotional material in boxes like the McDonald's all-time favorite Big Mac burger box. That was back when labels had money to spend on promo items, but that idea was beyond clever. It was the talk of the industry, and those acts were on fire.

When I started doing promotions at LaFace, I spent a lot of time in New York and California, and I took some ideas I saw in those markets and flipped them back to the Atlanta scene. I became one of the first label folks to have a wrapped van in that market. LaFace Records hit the streets, and we had an army of people (Taiye, Randal, Travis, Tommy and crew) passing out tapes, CDs, T-shirts, and more. We even shut down traffic on I-85 South during Freaknik, passing out Outkast promo materials. They were the most talked about group that weekend. We used a new approach to get the music out in a city that hadn't seen anything like it.

Also while I was working the Donell Jones project at LaFace, I made a CD sampler of his upcoming album and called it, "One for the Car, One for the Crib." I gave tastemakers two of the exact same CD so that they didn't have to drag the one from the car into the house. (yes pre-IPOD days). I hated having to switch out my CDs, but I loved listening to music while driving in my car AND while chillin' in the crib. The sampler caught on and became a huge buzz in the business, giving fans a double dose of the flavor. Another way of thinking out of the box!

I used another new approach when Outkast first went platinum, and we wanted to give them a party. Rather than do a typical party at a club, I threw a "Southernplayalistic Cookout/Concert." My intern Jaha Johnson (now one of Mary J. Blige's managers) hustled with me to make this an event unlike any other in the ATL. We rented a mansion in Decatur, Georgia, and set up a huge stage with bars and BBQ pits throughout the house and grounds and a dance floor outside. I was so nervous, and I really wasn't sure how this would end up. But it ended up a **huge** success. BET and MTV covered it, and the concert was one you would never forget. I had the following acts perform (all **before** they became huge stars): Outkast, Goodie Mob, Puff Daddy, Notorious B.I.G., Usher, and Busta Rhymes. All of Atlanta and New York came out. Things were lookin' up for the chick from southwest Atlanta. I was making a name for myself while remaining hungry and humble.

When you start experiencing the success and begin rising to the top, be careful not to toot your own horn too much. Black Moon asked, "Who got the props?" Even if you know you are killin' 'em and on top of your game, let others compliment you and sing your praises. You do not have to pop yo' collar! Be proud, but stay humble.

That will keep the ones who matter in your corner.

**LADIES, AS BRAND NUBIAN SAID, "EVERYBODY LOVES THE SUNSHINE."
BUT JUST WORK HARD, AND LET YOUR BRILLIANCE SPEAK FOR ITSELF.**

Kevin Liles and Shanti

Akon, Steve Rifkind, Shanti & Devyne at ATL Live on the Park

# CHAPTER TWELVE
## "CHECK THE RHIME"
### (Step Up to the Plate!)

Q-Tip said, "You on point, Phife? (Phife: "All the time, Tip") Then grab the microphone, and let your words rip!"

Ladies, don't be afraid to grab the mic and let yourself shine through your work. Always put your best foot forward. In this business, you can sometimes quickly rise to the top, but you have to be prepared for all there is to come. You cannot be afraid of the success/blessings coming your way! You also have to know how to handle it. As women, when we get into an executive position, we easily are pegged as either a bitch or NOT having enough "bitch" in us. I am not going to tell you which path to take. You have to find the approach that works for you.

Some of my other female mentors in the game exuded a lot more attitude and it worked for them, but that just wasn't my thing. I was more easygoing and humble. But that didn't mean I was a pushover. I'd never let anyone walk over me, and I was *always* prepared. Before walking into any senior staff meeting, I made it a point to go over agendas, sales info, marketing strategies—*everything*. The most embarrassing thing you can do is to not be prepared for a meeting. It looks bad to your team, and trust me, the boys in the room are keeping mental notes on how strong or weak you are.

Another thing to bear in mind as a woman is never to let them see you sweat in the office. Back in the day, there were more boutique labels,

and things were a little laid back. Now, fewer labels are in the marketplace, and those labels are major corporations run just like any other big business. Nelly said, it's getting "Hot in Here." But when you're feeling the pressure, hide it and be cool. You have to learn to play the politics and work twice as hard as your male counterparts do. When the goin' gets tough, the tough get goin'! You have to wear the pants and still be comfortable with your femininity.

Women are already perceived as emotional beings, so the worst thing you can do is make a business decision based on how you feel that day. And if someone makes you so angry in a meeting that you feel as if you could cry—well... **don't**! If you just can't take the pressure, ask to be excused. Step out, and go to the bathroom or go into your office and yell in a towel. Grandmaster Flash and the Furious Five said, "Don't push me 'cause I'm close to the edge, I'm tryin' not to lose my head, It's like a jungle sometimes it makes me wonder how I keep from goin' under." Just try to keep it together. Whatever you do, keep that po-poker face!

And **do not** buckle when someone yells at you. **Yes**, it's alot of yellers in the business that hold high positions. Let them get it out, then proceed with doing your job. I used to ignore the yelling, unless it got out of hand. And let's be clear...I never let anyone call me out of my name or blatantly disrespect me. Usually the yelling wasn't directed at me, just more about the situation. So learn to not sweat the tantrums and keep it movin'!

On another note, one of the most important things I learned early on from my mentors Antonio "LA" Reid and Kevin Liles was to brand myself. This was a great way to market myself in a big industry and get people to trust me for me, and not as Shanti Das from "dot dot dot." I learned to make "Shanti Das" a star.

So, I grabbed my mic and treated every project I worked on as the rap song of my life. I networked, took chances, and built the best lasting relationships in the business. I am proud to say I have an extensive Rolodex that will stay with me for years to come.

## LADIES, YOU CAN MAKE IT IN THIS BUSINESS, BUT YOU HAVE TO BE READY AND WILLING TO FIGHT THE GOOD FIGHT.

Dr. Cornel West and Shanti at Princeton University

# CHAPTER THIRTEEN
## "CAN'T TRUSS IT"
### (Beware of Politics as U-su-al)

Back in the day, Public Enemy told us that we "can't truss it!" Well, I'm here to tell you that, as a woman, a truer statement was never made.

We have to deal with so many issues on **all** levels in the workplace. Try salaries for starters. And this problem exists in all types of businesses, not just music. We can do the same jobs and still be underpaid. You have to research and dig deep to find out what the other boys are making. Truss **me**, if you don't ask for it, you will never get it.

Companies obviously want to make more and spend less. As I climbed the ladder of success, I found myself constantly getting less than my male counterparts did. I finally had to get a good attorney whom they would respect, just to get my higher-ups to take me seriously.

I remember when I moved from Atlanta to New York City in 2000, I was offered the exact **same** salary in New York that I was making in Atlanta. **Crazy!** I would have been living in a shoebox had I accepted those terms. I ended up taking other potential employer meetings with Sylvia Rhone at Elektra Records and Craig Kallman at Atlantic Records (thanks, Mark Pitts), until LA Reid finally stepped up and gave me a better offer than his original one at Arista Records.

You cannot take the first offer. They will always low-ball you. In contract negotiations, start high, so you can meet somewhere in the middle. No one is going to fight for you and your well-being better than you are. Understand the marketplace and the salaries of counterparts (both male and female) at various companies, and then equate that to your own value within the industry. That should help you determine a good salary. And know exactly what it is you bring to the table. If you have great relationships with your clients and artists, you are well worth the bigger paycheck.

Jay-Z made us understand that it's often "politics as u-su-al!" Another piece of politics that you should understand is that men turn the other cheek for their homies when it comes to side-hustles. I know so many guys who are heads of departments and have their own management companies and other businesses, but no one cares. Yet, when some women try to do more than their regular gig, World War II breaks out!

When we started R&B Live NY and some male executives at my company found out about it, I was questioned as if I was Lil Wayne making a "milli" a week. They ended up letting me do it (thanks, Sylvia, for holdin' me down), but it was crazy how they gave me the third degree. It wasn't a direct conflict of interest for the company. If anything, having one of their own at the helm of one of the hottest music events in New York City was a good look for them. I'm telling you this to let you know that it's up to you to always cover yourself. Keep "a few good men" **and** women on your side to help you sift through the bullsh*t.

It's important to add, though, that women can often be their own worst enemies in the workplace. Some of us will unfortunately throw each other under the bus because of intimidation, jealousy, or insecurity. So, as a woman dealing with other women, you have to be a good judge of character and know who has your back (you cannot truss everyone!). I can recall having haters in my own department, and I just continued to do my job and fought for the team. There is no "I" in team, and you have to learn to take the high road. In the end, make sure **you** do the right thing and do not succumb to evilinas in the room! Just kill 'em with kindness, and remember in business, it's about execution, not persecution. They will try to bring you down with them, but don't fall for it. I hope that, one day, **all** women will uplift each other, promote each other (those that truly deserve it), and not be afraid to support someone just as talented, if not MORE talented than they are. We should all want to find the next star to come behind us.

Last, don't expect everyone to help you, especially sometimes the ones in your company. Many folks "take care of their own." Be aware of your surroundings, and know who is down with whom. You do not have to kiss a*s, just be professional, but keep your eyes and ears open. And be aware of those that yes you to death, as they hate to be the bad guy. So, rather than helping you, they smile in your face and say yes, but never make good on their word. Many folks in this business will make promises, but never come through. Try not to make promises you cannot keep; you will lose a lot of respect doing that.

## LADIES, POLITICS IN THE WORKPLACE IS NOTHING MORE THAN "BEING SMART ABOUT HOW YOU MANAGE THE RELATIONSHIPS AT WORK." (MARIE G. MCINTYRE)

Shanti at the Proclamation Reception

Shanti at the WEEN Awards

Shanti at the Jay Z concert at Madison Square Garden

# CHAPTER FOURTEEN
## "THE CHOICE IS YOURS"
### (You Can Get with This, or You Can Get with That)

Black Sheep gave us the choice back in the day with that classic song. But those words still hold very true for women in the business. We can be a groupie or be a real fan; we can work our way to the top, or we can "sleep" our way to the top. The choice is yours, but I caution the ladies to think very carefully about those options. Given that we work in a highly social environment, it's inevitable that you *will* get hit on.

Now, nobody is saying that you cannot date folks in the business. It's typically not advised to date guys at your company, but if you do, **do it on your own terms.** That also goes for dating guys in the business in general. You must control the situation. It might be no one's business whom you date, but make sure to be a good judge of character and don't date a jerk. You must demand respect and make sure he really likes you and isn't just taking you for a ride. As I said, if you control the situation, you won't develop a reputation, and you won't get labeled "easy."

Turning a colleague or business associate into a boyfriend is one thing. But dating your boss is *not* recommended. Ladies, I don't care how fine he is. That leads to bad news every time. You want your boss to believe in you and to promote you based on business skills, not your bedroom skills. I hope that you are entering this business because you want to excel in your career, not to find Mr. Right. I don't need some dude to "powder blue, roc-a-wear-suit-white-NIKE me!"

It's not about that. It's about making your own money and building a life for yourself. Mixing business with pleasure is very tricky, and you should never expect anything from someone in the workplace if you choose to go down the social road. Be smart and be strong!

Dr. Dre made a song called "The Watcher." It's true that you never know who is watching. You cannot let your guard down when you are working in this game. Even when you leave the office and hang at parties with your other colleagues, you can't overdo it. It's not cute to get sloppy drunk in front of your peers. Been there, done that, and I learned quickly to put that on pause. I try to keep the social drinks to a minimum and wait until I am with my close friends who are not in the business to have a good time.

We also wake up every morning and make a conscious choice about what we will wear to work that day. So, choose right. We always need to dress the part. Please don't come to meetings with your "girls" out, and get mad when someone makes a comment about it. Remember, we work at an office and **not** at the club. The music industry is still a business first, and we have to act accordingly.

Try also not to be caught up with the hype of the talent and celebs. They are people just like you and me; they just have a few more dollar signs behind their names—smile. If you end up being friends with them, that's fine, but **do not** expect that. You can and will be burned. And if you are a true fan of their music, support them and help them to take their brand to a new level. Just do your j-o-b! They will respect you for your professionalism and for giving them their privacy. Be a worker-bee and not a groupie!

Last, rumors in this industry are inevitable. But we, as women, cannot get caught up in the lies and propaganda. Why would we want to keep perpetuating the madness and put each other down? Just mind ya' business, put your head down, and **work!**

## LADIES, LIKE RUN DMC SAID, "IT'S LIKE THAT, AND THAT'S THE WAY IT IS!"

Shanti's Shoe and Bag Game

# CHAPTER FIFTEEN
## "MO' MONEY MO' PROBLEMS"

(Gucci, Prada, Jimmy Choo—Manolo, Louboutin, and
Valentino too!)

Notorious B.I.G. and Puff Daddy tried to warn us that "mo' money" meant "mo' problems!" Well, I don't know about problems, but I can surely say that the more money you make, the more you spend.

It's great when you start making six figures and start getting a taste of those high-end goods. But it's all too easy to get caught up with wanting the hottest new designer jeans, shoes, or ridiculously expensive handbags. The sexy bags now range from $1,100 (Balenciaga) to $6,500 (Hermes Birkin bag). It's crazy how we want to keep up with the Joneses so we can look "so fresh and so clean!" Girl, we ain't the ones on stage singing or rapping, nor are we the ones walking the red carpet.

I can testify that I was once caught up. I had to have a new Roberto Cavalli dress for the Grammys and another one for the MTV or BET awards. My wardrobe wasn't complete without a new pair of Giuseppes, the Chanel bag (and matching wallet), and the Gucci shades. And all for what? Because I thought I had to look like the artists I worked with or the next hot chick at Label X. My colleague Hannah Kang put it best, "We're just buying excessive sh*t to stunt on people you couldn't give a damn about." Or we sometimes buy those items to find happiness in them. I finally turned it all over to **God** and let **Him** lead me to happiness.

Don't get me wrong. If you work hard, there is nothing wrong with rewarding yourself from time to time. But it makes no sense to overdo it. Looking back, I wish I had invested more of my money or even opened a few franchises. I could probably have six Papa Johns and five Subways at the rate I was spending.

The best advice I can give is to enjoy the good life but be smart about your money. Save, invest, and monitor your spending habits. As we all know, this music biz is experiencing some of the toughest times we've seen, and it might get worse before it gets better. Make sure you save some money for a rainy day. You never know when your label will make cutbacks and layoffs. When a company needs to shave from the fiscal budget, the first thing they do is look at overhead. Bodies are usually the first place they cut.

I have a saying from Sheila Coates, one of my colleagues in the business, that's fitting for this chapter: "Always have a little 'kiss my a*s money.' So that if you do get laid off or you feel the need to leave on your own accord, you have enough money to keep going as if you never skipped a beat!"

## LADIES, A PENNY SAVED IS A PENNY EARNED!

Shakir (Shake) Stewart, L.A. Reid, Babyface, KP,Dorsey and Shanti at L.A.'s wedding in Capri

Babyface, Shanti and L.A. at the '99 Superbowl in Miami

Lorraine Robertson, Eddie F, Phillana Williams, Sharliss Asbury, Michelle Montgomery and Shanti at the LAFACE reunion

GRAND GARDEN ARENA
MGM GRAND

Sharliss Asbury and Shanti in St. Bart's

B 207B 01
GATE SUITE ROW
SUITE LEU
Super Bowl
AFC-NFC WORLD CHAMPIONSHIP
SUNDAY, JANUARY 31, 1999 · 6:00

# CHAPTER SIXTEEN
## "GOOD LIFE"
### (It's Okay to Let Your Hair Down!)

Now, I know I just wrote an entire chapter about saving money and not overdoing it with the funds. But because this is such an intensely busy business and we work crazy hours, it is important to have a balance in your life. Kanye told us to enjoy the "good life!" It's all right to sometimes let your hair down and enjoy yourself. This business can afford you the opportunity to experience things that some people might never experience in a lifetime.

Back when the gettin' was good, some of my fondest memories came from being in this business. I can remember when LA Reid asked me if I wanted to join some staff in Los Angeles at the Soul Train Awards. *Are you kidding me?* I only grew up watching every episode of *Soul Train*. I savored every moment!

Then, there was the time when my good friend Sharliss and I flew to St Barts, several Diddy parties, and once flew on Diddy's private party jet to Miami. Priceless moments! Oh, and my good friend Sincere Thompson, Kevin Liles, and I drove in a car from Manhattan to Philly to attend the taping of Russell Simmons' *The Show*. Boy, that was hip-hop history for me! It was my first time meeting Kevin, and I had heard so many good things about him as an executive. Everyone I loved and admired in hip-hop was on that bill, and I had a back-

I can't forget about touring with Outkast back in the day and doing promo dates with Notorious B.I.G. He was so nice to me and was a big 'ole teddy bear. I was such a fan of his music and loved seeing him perform. When he had a tour date at Club Phoenix in my hometown, he told me I could stand on the side of the stage. Well, security swept the stage as they normally do before a big show. This huge guy literally picked me up and was going to put me down on the floor in the audience. But B.I.G. saw them disrespecting me and yelled, "No! Shoestring can stay!" And I rocked on the side of the stage the entire show, up close and personal with a hip-hop legend.

Dang! And the time LA and Babyface invited me to my very first NFL Super Bowl game. It was in Miami and my home team Atlanta Falcons were playing. Even though we lost, I had the time of my life. I've always been a huge football **Fanatic**. Oh, and I can't forget when LA had his 40th birthday party, and he had The Time perform…in his **backyard**! That was a Mastercard moment. Can't forget taking the SONY jet with Donnie Ienner and Michele Anthony to see Prince in rehearsal/concert—OMG! OK, I was about to forget about getting tickets to the Mike Tyson fights in the '90s (thanks, Craig Boogie). The Tyson vs. Holyfield fight is still one of the most talked about fights today.

Completey forgot to add the time when LA Reid shut down Barneys dept store an hour early before they closed in New York City for T-Boz and Chilli. It was like a scene from *Pretty Woman*. We were the only ones in the store along with the sales associates. They had one hour to grab as many clothes, shoes and bags as possible. I even ended up with a few trinkets (Prada bag, shoes, etc).

Finally, one of the greatest thrills was at Madison Square Garden when I saw Kanye West, Jay-Z, 50 Cent, Diddy, and Swizz Beatz—all on stage at the **same time**! It's all too easy to get jaded in this game. But experiences such as that were so special to me because I always remained a fan, both of the music and of the culture. Greatness was up there on that stage, and I got to bear witness. It was a moment in hip-hop history I could truly appreciate.

It's okay to kick it now and then, enjoy the perks, and have fun. You deserve to be there if you are focused and dedicated to winning.

## AS MCDONALD'S SAYS, "I'M LOVIN' IT!"

Shanti on the red carpet at the '10 BET Awards

# CHAPTER SEVENTEEN
## "WHATEVER YOU LIKE"
### (Dream BIG!)

T. I. once rhymed, "Baby, you can have whatever you like." Yes, you *can* have whatever you like from a business perspective, but only if you're not afraid to put the work in and go for the best of the best. With the success and expansion of the Internet, you now have tons of resources readily available. We didn't have the Internet or social media when I first got into the business. Now, you can get information faster, plan, start your own music blog or online radio talk show, and then some. The possibilities are endless.

Even when I didn't have all that, I never stopped putting in the work for the big payoff. While I was working at LaFace and doing my thing with Outkast, Goodie Mob, Usher, and TLC, there were times, however, when I felt as if I'd grown complacent with my paycheck and with my job title.

Steve Stoute, one of my mentors back then, taught me to want more for myself and to place a value on my abilities. Before Steve was a leading Brand Expert, he was managing Ras Passe, a group signed to LaFace and hustling for Interscope Records full time. Somehow, this guy managed to be everywhere.

Steve saw how I was on my grind and helped me to understand my value based on my contributions to the company. He even offered me a job in Los Angeles at Interscope and asked me to come over and run his street team department. The pay would be awesome, and I

had a tough decision to make. I knew I wanted a bigger salary, but I wasn't so sure about moving to Cali. Once LA Reid got wind of the situation, he stepped up and offered me more money to stay at LaFace. So, I took the increase in salary and duties and stayed in Atlanta.

But... I have to thank Steve Stoute for changing my thought process and understanding the brand equity that you build in yourself. He is one of the best at turning that equity into income.

You can always be more. When you find yourself coasting and every day on the job seems too easy or routine, it's time to shake things up and challenge yourself. And you do that by really understanding and appreciating what **you** are capable of and letting others know that you have so much more to offer.

Push yourself out of that comfort zone. You won't climb any higher unless you reach for it. As my good friend Johnnie Walker says, "You can't take the elevator to the top in this business, you gotta walk up the steps—one step at a time." And each step has a valuable lesson in it! So, no shortcuts and learn to appreciate the new challenges!

## LADIES, AS THE SUGARHILL GANG SAID, "SCREAM IT OUT AND SAY I AM—I AM, SOMEBODY—SOMEBODY!"